DEAD CATS DON'T MEOW

don't waste the ninth life

a collection of poetic wisdom for the discerning
(series 3)

TOLU' A. AKINYEMI

First published in Great Britain as a softback original in 2019

This revised and updated edition was published in 2021
Copyright © Tolu' A. Akinyemi

The moral right of this author has been asserted.

All rights reserved.

No part of this publication may be reproduced, stored in a retrieval system, or transmitted, in any form or by any means, without the prior permission in writing of the author, nor be otherwise circulated in any form of binding or cover other than that in which it is published and without a similar condition including this condition being imposed on the subsequent purchaser.

Design by Lola Betiku

LABET.MAKES.ART

Published by The Roaring Lion Newcastle LTD.

ISBN: 978-1-913636-17-3

Email:
tolu@toluakinyemi.com
author@tolutoludo.com

Website:
www.toluakinyemi.com
www.tolutoludo.com

ALSO BY TOLU' A. AKINYEMI

Dead Lions Don't Roar
(A collection of Poetic Wisdom for the Discerning)

Unravel Your Hidden Gems
(A collection of inspirational and motivational essays)

Dead Dogs Don't Bark
(A collection of poetic wisdom for the Discerning Series 2)

Dead Cats Don't Meow
(A collection of poetic wisdom for the Discerning Series 3)

Never Play Games with the Devil
(A collection of poems)

A Booktiful Love
(A collection of poems)

Inferno of Silence
(A collection of short stories)

Black ≠ Inferior
(A collection of Poems)

Never Marry a Writer
(A collection of poems)

Everybody Don Kolomental
(A collection of poems)

I Am Not a Troublemaker
(Children's Literature)

I Wear Self-Confidence Like a Second Skin
(Children's Literature)

A god in a human body
(A collection of poems)

DEDICATION

To my blooder – Olushola David Akinyemi, you are a warrior and victor – don't stop roaring.

Table of Contents

PREFACE 2
ACKNOWLEDGEMENTS 6

POEMS 11
MY STORY 13
DON'T CALL HER MUMMY 14
AUGUST FOURTEENTH 15
VALENTINE 16
CHILDREN OF NOWADAYS 17
AN ODE TO POETS 18
BRAIN BOX 20
AFRICAN WONDER 21
WHY I READ (1) 22
BLACK AND EXCEPTIONAL 23
CHANGE 24
BREAK THE JINX 26
DEAD CATS DON'T MEOW 27
ABUSE 28
SOUTH SHIELDS 29
A BLUE IN GEORDIE LAND 31
MISTAKE 33
RESOLUTION 34
PANGS OF ADULTERY 35
SILVER LINING 36
COLOUR BRAVE 37
PASSION 39
INTEGRITY 40
I AM BOOKTIFUL 42
SIX FEET 44
ONCE UPON A TIME 46

DEPRESSION AND SUICIDAL THOUGHTS	47
YOU ARE BOOKTIFUL	49
WHY I READ (2)	51
HAPPY WIFE, HAPPY LIFE	52
HUMILITY	53
EVERY DAY IS A SCHOOL DAY	55
ELECTIONS	57
THANK GOD IT'S FRIDAY	58
SPOKEN WORD	59
RAPED AT DAWN	61
HANDS OF TIME	64
TODAY	65
YESTERDAY	66
TWO IN ONE	67
HAPPINESS	70
HELLO BREXIT, SEE YOU LATER!	71
REALISTIC POET	73
SHHHHHHHHH	74
GLOBAL AUTHOR	75
NIGERIA	76
HUMANITY	78
SURVIVOR	80
YOUTHFUL EXUBERANCE	82
MUSINGS	84
EBOLA	86
COMPUTER VILLAGE	88
POLITRICK-IANS	90
CUSTOMER UNSERVICED	93
OJOTA PARK	95
MIRACLE	97
TWENTY-FIFTEEN	98
LAGOS TRAFFIC	99
OSHODI	101
BAD MARKET	103
MONEY LAUNDERING	105
DEADBEAT DAD	107
STIGMA	108
PAINED	110

THINGS WE SAY FOR LOVE 111
THE RANDY MAN 113
LIFE IS A TEACHER 116
HOME TRAINING... 117
RICH IN CASH, POOR IN PEOPLE............... 119
GALLANT WARRIORS 121
ONCE UPON A TIME (2)............................. 122
INGRATE... 125
GLASS HOUSE 127
CHRISTMAS 128
FRUITION... 130
ROCCAGORGA 131
CULTURE.. 133
MAGICAL 134
WISDOM 135
THIRTY-FIVE THOUSAND FEET 137
KING 140
DON'T ENVY... 141
CONTENDER 142
GOSSIP 143
TIT FOR TAT... 144
DEAD LIONS DON'T ROAR 2 145
EXHALE 147
MY WORDS 149

Bio **150**
Author's Note 153
Dead Lions Don't Roar 154
Dead Dogs Don't Bark 156
Dead Cats Don't Meow................................ 158
Unravel Your Hidden Gems......................... 160
Never Play Games with the Devil................. 162
A Booktiful Love 164
Inferno of Silence....................................... 166
BLACK ≠INFERIOR 168
NEVER MARRY A WRITER......................... 171
EVERYBODY DON KOLOMENTAL 173
A god IN A HUMAN BODY 175

I AM NOT A TROUBLEMAKER 176
I WEAR SELF-CONFIDENCE LIKE A SECOND
SKIN... 177

PREFACE

Dead Cats Don't Meow is my fourth published work, and third collection of my Poetry for the Discerning Series, after *Dead Lions Don't Roar* and *Dead Dogs Don't Bark*. It also follows my collection of inspirational essays, *Unravel Your Hidden Gems*.

    I hope you find some comfort in the poems in my latest collection, *Dead Cats Don't Meow*, and I sincerely hope that this book inspires you to put your best foot forward always. The after-effects of reading my poetry collections are profound, and my words will help you be at your creative best and spur you on to achieve greater things. My main aim with *Dead Cats Don't Meow* and the Poetic Wisdom for the Discerning Series is to nurture other budding talents to believe in themselves and put their enormous potential to great use.

Wherever you are reading my new collection, I am sure there will be something to take away, something new to learn from my repertoire of inborn wisdom. I have written these poems in the hope they will inspire you, yes YOU, that person reading this book – to put your gifts to use. You don't have to write a book; what's important is to put your peculiar gifts to use. Let's look at it this way: If Tolu' Akinyemi can do this, then you also can. In truth, you can even do better, in your own niche area with your distinct gift.

Dead Cats Don't Meow will help you find your own voice in a world with a cacophony of voices; it will teach you values and help you attain new heights. To the young person, it will help you face your fears boldly and conquer new grounds effortlessly. My books are life-changing, and they will leave you better; honestly, of what use is reading if it's not to gain new knowledge? As you can see, the trend in my poetry collections *Dead Lions Don't Roar* and *Dead Dogs Don't Bark* remains the same: We all have our unique roar, and permit me to add "bark". We are not just meant to be a statistic in the world population; we can be the change, the difference within our community, family and workplace.

Quit making excuses about lack of time; remember that everyone has twenty-four hours in equal proportion. Being busy should not be an excuse for not getting started.

Quit procrastinating as this has led to the death of many great ideas – many right before they were birthed. *Dead Cats Don't Meow* will help us find our "unique meow" in our everyday life, work, business, relationships, marriages, and it will help us put our talents to beneficial use.

In *Dead Cats Don't Meow: Don't waste the ninth life,* you will read poems that will inspire you to dance to your own rhythm, in your own unique voice. A cat has nine lives, but we might not have as many opportunities as a cat to have another go after the fall. "Don't waste your ninth life" is a clarion call – all of the opportunities that come our way throughout our life's journey should be harnessed; we should not wait for perfect conditions before we start that creative idea, sing that song, write that album and write that book. Only living cats meow; *Dead Cats Don't Meow*, so while you are here, let the world hear your own "unique meow"; don't be part of the numbers that spend their years in slumber.

As you go on to read through the pages of this book, which I have written especially for you, I do hope that you find it fulfilling and as great a read as it was a joy to write it.

ACKNOWLEDGEMENTS

Writing *Dead Cats Don't Meow: Don't waste the ninth life* was extraordinary as the Poetic Series for the Discerning is definitely here to stay. I have enjoyed great support from far and wide, and this is my opportunity to say thank you to the amazing people that have supported me during this process.

Thanks be to God Almighty for the intellectual ability to write another book and for giving me a voice to impact my generation positively. Thanks to my darling wife and partner, Olabisi – I appreciate the support at all times, as well as the epic banter, the candid advice, and for firmly holding down the homefront when I am away.

To the amazing and exceptional Isaac and Abigail; I am super proud to be your dad. You both are witty, intelligent, great readers, writers and lovers of the arts. I am happy I have inspired you positively and my prayer is that you will be greater than your parents in every way. Banish the negative voices in the world and don't be afraid to give expression to your talents.

My parents, Gabriel and Temidayo Akinyemi – you have been wonderful, selfless and so supportive. Thanks, super-dad and my ever-loving mum; words are not enough to say thank you for everything you have done for me. If I have the chance to come to the world again, I will gladly choose you booktiful ones to be the pilot over my affairs.

To my blooders Olusola and Oluseyi – I love you now and always; you both are destined for greatness.

To my one and only sister, Iretioluwa – There is no stopping you; the world is your footstool – go forth and conquer. My love to your kings, Segun and David.

Worthy of mention is Omotayo and Adedotun Adebiyi – I really do appreciate all of the support; I wish you lovelies continual success in all your endeavours.

A big thank you to Abiodun Coker for all of the support; we came right from the bottom, and now we are kinging. Big hugs to your darling wife, Moriam.

A special word of thanks to Deborah Jayeola, Emmanuel Osikilo, Karl Richardson, Nigel Rundle, Ayodeji Omogunsoye, Abi Oguntubi, Lanre Okanlawon, Abodunde Ojikutu, Wasiu Rabiu, Antonia Brindle (Get Brindled), Seye Morakinyo, Hakeem and Tessy Olagunju, Kashif Husain, Lekan Owoeye, Olugbenga Obakin, Oladapo Arofin, Daniel Williams, Ijeoma Ucheibe (The Bagus), Bandele Okunowo, Anthonia Brown, Oloyede Michael Taiwo (Philo Baba), Mustapha Apooyin, Bartholomew Akinwale and Adewale Ogunbadejo (Legover).

Thank you to Ian Mcalister for your constant support and my "guy" Yinka Abubakiri – you are top notch. A big shoutout to Chris Horsborough for the fantastic ideas on the book covers.

Special thanks to Lola Betiku for designing amazing book covers. And to my editors, Hungry Bookstore and Adeola Juwon Gbalajobi. It's always a pleasure working with you.

Final appreciation and shout out to my good friend – Daniel Dada; we have come a long way together, and oh well, we are roaring in the right direction. I appreciate all the little gestures and you always looking out for my good.

POEMS

MY STORY

Hear my story and be inspired.
When I say *au revoir* in years to
    come,
Tell them about Tolutoludo
    Akinyemi,
who came to Newcastle with dreams
    and grit and left positive imprints
    on the sands of time.
Tell them he came in the form of a man, but he
    was a lion.
Tell them he was a man of action and he stood
    by his words no matter whose ox is gored.

Tell them he was not afraid of standing
    against the crowd for he was bold
    and fierce.
Tell them also the story of his fails;
do not shroud his weakness in odes.
Tell them of his bruises and the stormy
    seas he cruised.
Tell them his story unabridged.

DON'T CALL HER MUMMY

Don't call my wife *Mummy*.
She is young and bubbly with youth.
Don't call my wife *Mummy*.
If you were never her suckling,
don't make her feel like an old soul
trapped in the web of a young body,
lest you see me fuming with rage.

Inspired by Pst. Akinkunmi Thomas

AUGUST FOURTEENTH

A memorable day, the day a gem was born.
Allow me to blow her horn, for virtuous
    women like her are rare.
Words are not enough to describe her worth;
    she weaves dreams into being – a
    matriarch at home, a boss at work.
Darling, you are lovable, adorable, reliable and
    dependable.
    You are the blessing of my life.
You eased my burden in the days when it was
    tough, when life was rough, when all we
    saw was a glimmer of hope.
You lent me your strength and invested your
    faith in me, and for this, I will write your
    name in gold.

For my queen – Olabisi

VALENTINE

Valentine's was once a day we raised the banner of love,
but it's become a day we unleash our lust.
It was once a day for pure affection,
but we tore its fabric, ripping off the innocence of the blessed day.
Valentine's became a day we feed our lustful appetite,
instead of reflecting and expressing perfect love.

CHILDREN OF NOWADAYS

Children of nowadays are intelligent and savvy – the epithets of exceptional minds.

Questions upon questions: *Daddy, why, why and why?*

They are what I desired to be as a youngster: inquisitive, curious and challenging.

Inspired by Isaac & Abigail Akinyemi

AN ODE TO POETS

We are the unsung heroes, the unheralded firemen that puts out the smoke billow.

We are the uncelebrated players, a league one, hat-trick, scoring striker on television, fighting for the media's attention.

We are brave hearted, like assorted outfits sold in an unknown market.

We are poets, slammers, open micers – feel free to call us fighting tigers.

We are the forgotten genre fighting our way back to the bookshelf.

We are a major force, no longer begging on all

fours.

We are poets.

To all poets worldwide – don't stop roaring.

BRAIN BOX

Ideate and create; discover your inner talent.

You have so much latent skill and potent power; don't let anyone belittle you.

Remember, you are a giant; you are radiant with possibilities.

Keep your creative juices alive.

You are a brand, a brain box of ideas.

AFRICAN WONDER

Heroine, goddess – a true African Woman.

Say: wonder woman.

Serenade her with soothing words.

Royalty, fierce – African wonder.

This African beauty needs no embellishment.

Call her *the African Queen.*

WHY I READ (1)

I would have been an empty barrel,
a toothless bulldog in a gated mansion.
I would have drowned in the ocean of ignorance,
besotted with a poverty of ideas.
But I read, hoping someday I will be a scholar,
a bright star amongst my peers, my footprints etched in folklore, remembered for greatness and good works.

Inspired by The African Writers

BLACK AND EXCEPTIONAL

I am Black, Black and exceptional.
I am free from limitations;
I refuse to be an imitation.
I am Black, Black with pride.
No longer shackled in the closet,
the world sees me as an asset.

I am Black; don't adorn me with a label:
Black African, Black American, African American, Jamaican or Caribbean, Black British.

I will always remember my history.
I am Black, Black and exceptional.

CHANGE

We hanker in solitude;

We ponder and resist change
   with our might.

We fight for the
habitual, for we are
lovestruck with the perpetual.

We are prickly,
bodies itchy for the new-
fangled.

We are entangled in the
   ancient ways;
we become reticent when we
hear transformation.

We resist the revolution,
   arms across our chests,
ready to fight with our war
chest.
We have our carol, well-versed

cantos,

all to resist change.

BREAK THE JINX

How do you break the jinx of mediocrity?
How do you wipe out the label, local champion?
How do you transition from your locality to a global stage?
Without going viral in a controversial way?

See every failure as a springboard to success.
Embrace your vulnerability and pain.
Celebrate your little victories like a ground-breaking feat.
Give every audition your best shot, and never drift into slumber in the place of preparation.
Treasure these words like a prized asset; never be in haste like a plane over-shooting its runway.
This is how to break the jinx of mediocrity.

DEAD CATS DON'T MEOW

A cat has nine lives.

The cat's meow is a signal of its life.

Dance to your rhythm; find your unique voice.

Don't waste the ninth life,

the opportunities hidden in dust.

You can be the hero;

let the world hear your meow.

Chase your dreams.

Don't waste those golden chances;

the world is a stage – act your part.

Don't get lost in the seas of heads,

like a herd of wandering cattle without a herdsman.

Give it your best performance;

don't waste the ninth life.

ABUSE

The words we say without a thought
show our lack of grace,
and words, once spoken, are like
shattered eggs; they cannot be gathered.
Verbal abuse is a killer;
an abusive relationship
kills slowly, like a poison.
Abuse breaks the core of the soul.

Abuse sent me to a faraway land
where I can breathe,
live in peace and be free.

SOUTH SHIELDS

On the 25th of August 2018 in
    South Shields, near the high
    seas, rustling birds flying
    across the evening skies,

a stranger sitting on a bench
    beckoned to me. The voice
    rang out: *Please pray for me.*
    Pray for my leg, he begged.

I was bewildered. *Why me?* I
    pondered.

I did the honours – spoke words of
    healing over the legs and
    hoped my faith made him
    whole.

His face glowed in gratitude.

Malcom was the man,
an angel in flesh and blood.
Our paths might never cross
    again,

but I left him with my words, my
>   gift to the world.
He left me with the truth and
>   some words to soothe.

On the bench in South Shields, I
>   met an angel
I won't forget in a lifetime.

To the Angel I met in South Shields on the 25th of August 2018.

A BLUE IN GEORDIE LAND

Circled in the midst of Geordies,
    Newcastle versus Chelsea was the match
I was the catch with chants I took as bants.

My offence was wearing blue –
this could leave me bruised.

Chants of *rent boys, rent boys, rent boys* filled the air,
but there was no need to fear.
I chanted back: *Geordie, Geordie, Geordie!*
I had no plans to leave in panic.

I was playing my cards and the home lads gave me a free pass.

Don't hide; it's okay to swim against the tide and
go along for a ride.
As long as you swallow your pride,

you can always come out a king and retell the adventures of a blue in Geordie's Land.

My adventure during a premier league match between Newcastle and Chelsea at St. James' Park on the 26th of August 2018.

MISTAKE

Everybody makes mistakes.
Give me a chance to retake,
See this as a blunder.
Don't let it put our friendship asunder.

Your anger seems like thunder.
Don't let this linger; forgive and forget.

Let love beam again.

RESOLUTION

We start January, beaming with hope and faith in new prospects,
but as the months pass by,
the dreams, visions, and those lofty goals wither away like falling leaves in winter.

Haunted by the ghost of our failings,
we recycle dreams
till we have the chance to write another New Year's resolution.

PANGS OF ADULTERY

Putting fire in your bosom will get you burned.

Why play with fire?

Why soil the vow you took before God and men?

A quickie can leave you needing a quick fix.

Marriage is sacred; don't let another person see you naked, as this could leave you tainted,

making your life complicated.

Adultery is a fool's sport;

it leaves one with pangs of regret.

SILVER LINING

See the silver lining in the blue skies.
No matter how tiny,
see the sun rays, believe –
tomorrow will bring exculpation.
Sorrow is fleeting.
Don't relent;
keep striving and someday
you will see the silver lining.

COLOUR BRAVE

I am the colour
brave.
I refuse to cave in to
typecast
bias because of my colour.
Don't let disparity thrive
in a season of equal
opportunities.
Let's bin the echoes of
injustice of years past.
Don't treat me as an
outcast;
be colour-blind.
I have a voice;
don't suppress it.
The unending narratives
about discrimination
and disenchantment,
let's put a stop to them.
Celebrate my individuality
and uniqueness.
All lives matter should be
the new mantra

and watch the world become a better place.

PASSION

Follow your passion,
the course that seems noble
above everything else.
Follow your dreams, not
the crowd;
don't get on the bandwagon.
You deserve to be happy.

INTEGRITY

Our hands are soiled with dirt and mud; we are tainted with earth and dust.
We have lost our voice,
values
and moral standing.
We dined with the devil;
our ways are evil.
We go to equity
with unclean hands.
Our conscience has been
    buried in the dawn of the
    day.
We are at our lowest ebb,
    caught in the web
of corruption and
    perverseness.
We claim to be holy,
    but act ungodly.
We have elevated
mammon over and
above all.
Men are now our gods;

we are religious,
yet vicious; we do nothing,
and nevertheless, expect miracles.
We have thrown integrity
    to the gutters.
Our hearts are the corridors of hell.
We cut corners and chase the fast life.
We loathe orderliness and uprightness.
We reap where we do not sow,
leaving heartbreaks in tow.
We are the lost generation;
I hope this causes a
repentance, touches the core
of your soul.
Don't play foul,
without integrity when it comes
    to the nitty-gritty;
stand for integrity and
    keep standing.

I AM BOOKTIFUL

I am booktiful; flip through my pages.
I am not a statue to adorn your bookshelf, untouched.
Treasure me – I am a spring of ideas.
I won't leave you the same.
Don't be part of the ignorant throng throwing out the ridiculous parlance: *I don't read.*

Knowledge is power; knowledgeable folks stand strong like a tower.
Ignorance is a malady!
Be booktiful – serenaded by words.
Be a reader if you aspire to be a leader.
The writer who doesn't read is like a car running without fuel.
Be booktiful – besotted with paperbacks like a lovestruck

couple on a first date.

Expand your knowledge base.

Flip through, read it,

get soaked in – be booktiful.

Written to celebrate all booktiful people all over the world.

SIX FEET

Our arrival was heralded with tears
of joy
(for some, it was hurt and sorrow).
Our departure will be heralded
with tears,
sorrow and pain.
This place has never been home;
it wasn't meant to be.
We lost our way, forgetting it was
transient.
All our earthly treasures, the
pleasures
and lures of the world – now
distant memories.
We lived in big houses
We came empty and we'll be
returning empty – some
charred with ashes as a
remembrance,
others wrapped up in a tiny little
sarcophagus.
Remember it all ends someday,

six feet down below.

See this as an audition;

act your part

with all of your heart;

give it your best shot.

Sow happiness.

Be kind to others.

Leave good memories.

Rewrite your story.

Let someone be thankful

all because you came into the world.

ONCE UPON A TIME

I have heard words that made my heart melt,
tasted love that was sincere,
been treated like a dove, doted on.
I was once someone's sweetheart.
Once upon a time,
I was swept off my feet,
served breakfast in bed
by a woman to die for.
Now all that remains of those times are memories.

DEPRESSION AND SUICIDAL THOUGHTS

There are times you feel alone,
heavy, laden with so much
    burden,
like the four pillars carrying the
    weight of a gigantic building.

Your thoughts are filled with
    darkness and demons haunt
    you.
But know you are not alone.
You're not the only one going
    through the tedious hills of
    life,
wishing for rest in the arms of
    death.

Listen, friend – ignite a passion for
    life and soak your mind in a
    stream of positive thoughts.
Don't be drowned in the ocean of
    self-pity;
depression is regressive analytics;

you don't want it in your
    mathematical formulae.

Perish those suicidal thoughts,
snuff them out,
breathe,
you deserve to be happy and alive
    again.

YOU ARE BOOKTIFUL

You are booktiful; don't
act pitiful.
You are a queen with a
   lively mien.

You are a king with
   treasures to bring;

You are talented and
relentless.

Everyone has their season
   - your time will soon
   come.

You will experience a
boom.

Nothing lasts forever,
not this sorrow and
failures.

Keep hope alive; go for

your goals.

Go all out for your dreams; forget the pipe-dreams.

Shut out the naysayers.

You are booktiful like a snow-filled road on a winter morning.

Honey, I repeat, *you are booktiful.*

"*Booktiful*" *is a term used by the author as a substitution for beautiful.*

WHY I READ (2)

Reading was the wiper blade that wiped my slate clean from the cesspit of mediocrity.
Reading was my shield,
my life jacket.
In the days of unending turbulence,
reading took me on the path of self-discovery,
my intelligence barometer forever increased.
Reading left me booktiful.

Inspired by The African Writers

HAPPY WIFE, HAPPY LIFE

The key to a happy life is to be
connubial with a happy wife.
A happy wife means less strife.
We all resent tantrums splashed
around like overflowing water.
A happy wife is the recipe for a
peaceful home,
a clear head and great strides.
Many homes are like a ship about
to hit an iceberg;
a wife can break or make.
Every king needs a queen – this
is not a fallacy, or enticing words;
this is the password to a happy life.

Inspired by David Wilson – thanks for the constant prompts.

HUMILITY

Humility was the missing armour in the war-chest of Adebayo's daughter.
Humility was sent on an errand to the land of no return.
Adeshola had all the traits of a beauty queen, but her good character was sent to exile.
Her attitude was in deficit like an overdrawn account exceeding its credit limit.
Respect was a non-existent vocabulary word in the dictionary of this queen whose only claim to the crown was beauty.
But of what use is beauty without a pleasant attitude?
Character is the crown that makes beauty perfect.

Adebayo, also spelled Adébáyọ̀, is a Yoruba name which either means "he came in a joyful time", or "the king/crown/royalty meets joy".

Adeshola is a unisex Nigerian name which translates to "Crowned for Wealth, Bring Wealth Home, Royalty," in English. It is common among the Yoruba tribe in Nigeria.

EVERY DAY IS A SCHOOL DAY

Every day is a school day,
an opportunity to increase knowledge.
Every day is a learning curve,
a chance to wave ignorance off.
No one is an island, a
 repertoire of all
 wisdom.
Embrace learning,
 education and
 constant
 improvement.
Let old ideas die;
 innovate, embrace
 the new,
hoping someday you
 will be one of the
 select few
smiling on payday all
 because you
 envisioned every day
 as a school day.

Inspired by David Wilson – thanks for the constant prompts.

ELECTIONS

Elections are looming
Vague promises are booming
Brooms are selling
Beware of fake notes,
sorry, change,
leaky umbrellas
and our politicians.

THANK GOD IT'S FRIDAY

Hurray, it's Fri-yay!
Our expectations so copious,
we're looking forward to a weekend of fun.

Thank God it's Friday –
our smiles are different.
Warm handshakes and hugs speak in different tongues.

Our plans articulated,
the weekend begins in earnest –
a time to unwind from all the stress
that permeated the week.

Everyone loves a Friday.
Some say it is the best day of the week.
Little wonder it was deserving of this poem.

SPOKEN WORD

Your spoken word
    shapes your world.
Your spoken word is the
    genesis and the
    revelation of your life.
Your spoken word is the
    catalyst
of your life,
the successes and
    failures.
Some embrace positivity;
    others thrive in
    negativity.
You get in measure the
    harvest of your
    spoken word.
Be careful of the words you
    speak;
don't let anyone sow negative
    words in your life.
Serenade yourself with
    positive pronouncements
    and watch yourself thrive

in the midst of chaos.

Be careful of the words you speak and let people speak to you.

RAPED AT DAWN

We were raped at dawn.
What remains of the big turkey is a mere carcass.
Our country has been left in tatters by the leaders who should superintend it.
We are the beautiful bride deserted on the wedding day by the groom.
They deceived us with their brooms and the shout of change.
Herdsmen, cows and their ilk have become lords of the animal farm.
We are the butt of all jokes, fairy tales
of animals devouring money like a hungry man with a ravenous appetite.
Our looters have gone berserk,
the commonwealth frittering for bogus projects.
Our senators are dancers and musicians and are in the habit of clowning.
Our hallowed chambers are no longer sacred,
the louts in *agbada* have turned them to boxing rings,

fighting over money to launder;
chairs thrown for fun, mace stolen,
minority members impeaching the majority
–

a sitcom that makes for hilarious viewing.
Corruption is our companion;
some said stealing was not corruption.
We refused to kill corruption and now it is
    killing us on our roads due to potholes,
the blood of the masses spilled, leaving
    unending heartache in tow.

Our godfathers and party leaders have
    gone *mental;* they anoint, de-anoint
    and appoint whoever they feel is
    deserving.
Our votes no longer count.
Somewhere in Bourdillon, a lion has
    haemorrhaged our future for his own
    allures.
Our politicians have no values or ideals.
They camp, decamp and
take power for their own
interests.

Our anti-corruption fight is
    selective;
the paraphernalia of the
    office has been used
    against the opposition.
    The people no longer
    matter.
How did we get here?
Did we get the leaders we
    deserve?
Will ours ever be a great
    nation?
When will our jungle mature
    and be free from these
    vultures, these animals
    in the form of men
who raped us at dawn, took
    away our honour, glory
    and prestige?

HANDS OF TIME

I wish I could turn back the hands
of time, reset the clock of my life
so I can forget all the snags
    and plagues
that beset me.

I wish I could turn back the hands
of time,
start with a clean slate,
another chance to determine my
fate,
write a new story,
miming to a victory song
with the world cheering.

I wish I could turn back the hands
    of time,
undo all the errors of my past and
    have
another chance
to take a lap of honour.

TODAY

Today is my only chance
    at survival.
I will treat today like a prized
ornament. Today is my chance
to start afresh,
be abreast
and re-write my story
with renewed hope.

Today is my opportunity to
put my gifts to use
by being creative,
    productive and avant-
    garde.

Today is the chance
I have to re-write my
future,
another chance to dream,
    fight and live.

YESTERDAY

Yesterday is history; the pain,
sorrow and worry are all
in the recycle bin.

Yesterday is dead with
its fiascos.

Yesterday drowned my fears,
my flaws
and weaknesses.

Yesterday is gone, never to return,
never to be seen again.

TWO IN ONE

The wedding bells
ringing aloud,
we were told the two have
become one, the rings
exchanged.
Seems more like a
ritual,
a practice now
habitual.
What we hear now:
Is your ring diamond,
gold
or silver?
We are enthralled by how
    many gold-carat ornaments
    adorn our fingers.
We have been enchanted by the
    wedding ceremony; we give no
    thought for the marriage.
    Hence, we see marriage as a
    bondage.
We are married but single;
once in a while, we still want

to mingle. Devoured by our
exes like Pringles,
we still want the occasional
tickle
that might leave us red-
faced. Marriage is now
over-rated;
this leaves me frustrated.
In an age when feminism
 seems top-rated, I believe
 in human rights
 and woman-rights
 and a happy
 home.
But the standards are
falling;
the centre no longer
holds.

The two cannot be one when
 marriage is seen as a
 competition,
an opportunity to flex
 muscles
as if we are opposing figures

    in a boxing ring,
threatened by each other's
success, daggers drawn in
disharmony.

This is turning into an unholy
matrimony; your suits,
wedding gown
and the budget of your
    wedding will long be
    forgotten;
no one will remember in years to
come
the glitz and glamour
of the wedding party
in the aftermath of a crumbled home.

HAPPINESS

Your happiness is within your grasp; stop looking for affirmation
and acceptance from
    all and sundry.

No one is responsible
for your joy;
it's your responsibility to celebrate
the little feats and accomplishments.

HELLO BREXIT, SEE YOU LATER!

Brexit

>was the shambolic exit.

>Migrants,
>treated like an unwanted species;
>we refuse to be our brother's keeper.

Brexit

>was the pill that left the bitter taste.
>*Leave or remain.*
>*Deal or no deal.*
>It won't be the same.

Brexit

>took away our rights.
>We lost our freedom, trade deals,
>jobs
>and our togetherness.

Brexit

>was a child of circumstance,
>the implosion
>of our ignorance right in our faces.

Brexit

    will never be forgotten

    in our history books,

    the singular event that left us all shocked, starring

    the pusillanimous Cameron,

    the chronicles of Farage and UKIP's fear-mongering,

    the indecisive May.

    Bo-Jo was a renowned traitor;

    Corbyn lost his voice,

    with the Tories left in disarray.

Brexit

    was the exit,

    the unwanted child of circumstance

    thrust on us by fate,

    politicians and ignorance.

REALISTIC POET

I am a realistic poet.

You can't detach the bard
from poesy.

Rhymesters and verse are like
bread and butter.

My words,
written and spoken are
bespoke;
they are a creation of my flora
and fauna – enjoyment, mirth,
disappointment, grief and
waterworks.

I am a realistic poet; I ooze
creativity.
My words are birthed from a
place of scrupulousness,
truth
and savoir faire.

I am a realistic poet;
my words can be your reality.
Inspired by Realistic Poetry

SHHHHHHHHH

Don't let anyone belittle your achievements.

You didn't get to the top by accident;
    you paid the price
    and you deserve the prize.

Don't let anyone keep you quiet.
You have not come this far to
give in
to those voices
that strive to disparage
and underestimate
your accomplishment.

GLOBAL AUTHOR

I am a global author.

Some call me local, but
I have crossed borders,
traversed oceans.
I have been given shelter
in homes I never thought I
could step in. My words
have been comfort
to people of different colours.

I am a global author.
This is not grandstanding;
I know my onions.
I have the nous and charisma.
I know my worth
and I am confident in my journey.
There is a bestseller in me.
Feel free to call me a global author.

NIGERIA

Nigeria was the greatest,
the most populous.
We have been led by the most ridiculous. Nigeria is a castrated dog,
stationary like wallpaper art,
the mincemeat of the rogues
we call leaders.
Nigeria is an aberration;
we are united in our dysfunctional state.
We pray and pray,
yet tomorrow still brings the same.
Our PEPs are notorious;
they bleed the coffers
and in truth have nothing to offer. Nigeria was the beautiful bride
whose lot was an abusive groom.
Nigeria is the giant of Africa.
At independence, we thought it

was eureka;
it has been a hit and miss.
We hope someday our flag will be held aloft in pride,
our nation the most desirable
to live on Earth.

Inspired by Linorajj.com

PEP is an acronym for "Politically Exposed Person".

HUMANITY

I still believe in humanity,
    The good in humans,
    the humane touch,
    the support systems,
    the ones that give us a shoulder to lean on,
    the nameless doctors
    on a night shift rota,
    the ambulance drivers that use
        their dexterity to navigate
        through the testing rush-hour
        traffic,
    the anonymous blood donors –
    Let's call them
    "lifesavers" – the organ
    donors
    who have died selflessly.
    Humanity is not
        apropos of the
        dough stacked up
        in your bank

account;
humanity is the act of
giving
and letting go.

I still believe in humanity,
the caregivers
who do their all to ensure
    that we get the best
    care.
Humanity has taught me
    that love is more
    important than money.
The leaders who gave shelter to the
    victims of war, opening their
    borders
to give them a new lease of
life –
that's humanity.

The whole essence of our
    journey is giving, sharing
    and loving.
When I lose all hope,
I won't lose hope in humanity.

SURVIVOR

This is a story of hope,
to keep believing
in the face of despair.
This will touch you to the marrow –
It moved me too.
There are some battles I never expected to fight; fighting over dollies
at two years old would have been a joy, displaying the famous naughty two tantrums
– that might have been a dream,
but here I am at two years old,
in my innocence;
I have fought and won
a battle no one could ever have predicted –
cancer of the liver.
Don't cry me a river –
I am now a victor.

This is a story of hope,
of healing,
of believing and fighting.
I faced the biggest battle of my life
at two. What is your excuse?
You can't give up now;
you can't stop believing;
you can't stop fighting.
Cancer was defeated.
I am a survivor,

a hope-giver.
I hope my story gives you hope
in your weakest moment
and comforts you.
Never ever give up.

Dedicated to Toyosi Aromire

YOUTHFUL EXUBERANCE

Plucking the guava fruit from Amaka's father's garden is a vivid memory of youth that has lasted a lifetime.
The freshly served Jollof
> was the victim of my youthful dexterity –
always up to no good.

Sagging trousers,
like those worn by underfed prisoners;
flying collars are the ultimate symbol of
> the unbreakable energy of youthful vigour.

In these days,
youthful exuberance might
> have changed the
paraphernalia of its office,
but the application still remains the same.

My church mind tells me

  that youthful exuberance is
exaggerated,
    a concoction of our innovative
    minds ready to take on the
    world
    like an explorer on a tour.

    And someday we will outgrow
it,
    laugh in sheer amazement
    at the actions that made us feel
    superhuman.

  Amaka is an Igbo name for girls, meaning "beautiful".

MUSINGS

There is no manual to be a good mother; compassion was not taught as an elective course.

In the world's best business school,
no one teaches a woman how to
carry her pregnancy for nine months
or the best methodology to push through a baby on delivery day.

We are all day-trippers, greenhorns
in the journey of life, crisscrossing the universe. Life has taught us lessons
in unimaginable dimensions.
The hard-hearted became meek
when life's storms hit.
There is no manual to go to bed;
neither is there an anecdote for a

bitter person
than to give them some
recipe
from the cookbook of love.

EBOLA

The Ebola virus gripped the heart of our nation. Like an unwelcome sojourner, it wandered, looking for where to perch
and put us on the
brink of destruction;
ostracization from the
comity of nations.
Ebola gave birth to a heroine –
Stella Adadevoh was our knight in shining armour.
She was patriotic,
saving us from the catastrophe.
The impact would have been of monumental proportions. We have lost one of the few valiant ones
who stood gallant to the
very end;
she was one of a kind.

Written in memory of Dr Ameyo Stella Adadevoh – to celebrate her bravery and gallantry at great cost to her life.

COMPUTER VILLAGE

A village owned by computers,
aptly put.
Computers are permanent residents in
   this awkward village
in Ikeja, right in the heart of Lagos, the
   centre of excellence.

The Computer Village is the home of
   technology gadgets and everything
   smart.
The major attribute to exhibit
   is street credibility.
This will save you from a languid visit
that could ultimately leave you as a
   wailing wailer.

The Computer Village is the first of
its kind. Hoping someday we have
other villages, like
   phone villages,
television villages and
   their ilk,
inhabited by inhuman

artefacts, the lust of our extravagances
and appetite for everything worldly.

The Computer Village is the largest ICT accessory market in Africa.

POLITRICK-IANS

Politricks is a well-remunerated job in our nation.

How well can you recount the tale of an unknown fella
with a dodgy source of wealth
becoming an overnight billionaire?
That was pulled off from the trick bag of our politrickians with slogans and mantras that will make the dead shiver. They are at an equilibrium with mediocrity,
being static is second nature.
They fleece the Commonwealth in gargantuan proportions; their conscience has been buried
in the mire of corruption.
Politricks is a game of number and magic –
the more you look, the less you see.
Our politricks has been infiltrated by saboteurs;

our politrickians took the devil to
    lunch,
gave him a nice habitation
    and have been gracious
    hosts. Our politrickians
    fight dirty,
blood on their hands.
You can't tell on which part of the
    divide they belong – for the state
    or against the state.
They host unholy meetings in the dark
    of the night,
building alliances to line their pockets.
Since independence, we have had bitter
    tales; corruption and
    underdevelopment are part of our
    hegemony.
Our politrickians' DNA is so strong –
decades after decades, they
keep replicating their kind.

Politricks is a game of tricks
    I can't unearth with a
microscopic lens. Politrickians
keep us in deep slumber and

perpetual slavery.

Politrickians was coined for this poem as a term for politicians playing tricks on the governed.

CUSTOMER UNSERVICED

In saner lands,

customers are treated like royalty –
respected and esteemed.

In my motherland, the customer is treated like garbage.
Our customer service is dysfunctional;
the service we offer is appalling,
year after year, we break our own records.
This is not utopia.

Our welcome smiles
have been discoloured by the anguish and pain of the failed system.
We gravitate towards the unusual,
holding the customer ransom,
after all we can choose to un-service the customer with no questions to answer.

No one calls us to order.

Good customer service is a pipe dream, a dream that came to pass in a distant land where customers are treated like kings.

OJOTA PARK

Humans shackled in rickety
buses,
    the type that have missed their
        sell-by date by decades.
Touts showing their clout,
beckoning passengers with
    bellowing sounds.
Road safety was a lullaby.
Passenger welfare was at best a
lowly rank.
No soothsayer was needed to
foretell this –
the billowing smoke from cigars
    and lips darkened with *Sapele*
    water sputtered down in gulps
    told the whole story,
like our much-loved super-story
    on prime-time television.
The famous dump site was an
    epitaph, a solemn reminder
    and a companion of our
    famous Ojota Park –
a scented reminder to

    ubiquitously
welcome us to Lagos
and a souvenir to remind us of the
    good and bad side of the
    beautiful Lagos.

Sapele water is a locally brewed alcoholic beverage with herbal extracts.

MIRACLE

Don't tell me to pray for a
    miracle when you can be
    my miracle.
You welcome me to your basilicas
    with open arms; your academes
    are beyond my wherewithal.
Every generation has its own
    revolutionary symbol, a martyr
Don Freeze might not adorn
that toga, but he has been the
truth
that we have been blinded from
seeing.
We have lived in denial,
the truth staring at our sombre faces
    in bemusement. We are at a
    crossroad,
when we refuse to touch the
    revered, the man who lives
    in the celestial realm, an
    angel in human skin
who can do no wrong.

TWENTY-FIFTEEN

Twenty-fifteen was supposed to be the end of
　　the amalgamation, an unholy
　　matrimony,
a union of strange bedfellows thrust upon us
　　by selfish colonial masters.
How can you lump together atypical people?
The tales of disunity have been our
swansong,
tribalism and sectionalism
boldly written on our faces.
They wanted us to be on the precipice,
our oil up for grabs,
our land in turmoil
and our politicians willing accomplices.
It was easy to predict our demise –
the obituary of the pride and giant of Africa.
Lest they forget we are fighters,
we refuse to dance to their drumbeats
and sounds of war,
leaving them like hallucinated journeymen.
They swallowed their spittle, pride and
predictions
and await another doomsday.

LAGOS TRAFFIC

Lagos traffic is a gentle reminder of
our lost manners,

productive hours wasted in the
dawn of the day, precious family
time buried in the cool of the
evening.

Lagos traffic is a testament that we are
a people without laws, our ways
are amoral.
Immediately after the Sunday
Ecclesiastical service and Friday
Jumaat,
we act like unchained
dogs, vociferous and
ready to prowl.
Driving against traffic is now the
norm.
Uniformed men acting like un-
informed citizens –
what a parody.
We are all in haste against rush-hour
traffic.

Lagos traffic is the antonym of sanity,
vendors of all wares encumbering
the free flow of traffic,
unaccounted for revenues in
the millions and the odd
knick-knacks snatchers,
thieves and hordes of
criminals
hiding under the canopy of
darkness and the retreating
sunshine.
Lagos traffic is a behest of
activities, one of a kind,
which can only be found in Lagos City.

OSHODI

The big molue buses were the true symbol of Oshodi before the famous BRT buses
overshadowed and thrust them into the land of the forgotten.
Unlicensed pharmacists and doctors were August visitors, the sticking point of a molue ride
with drugs that can cure all manner of sicknesses. Before Dora brought her aura
and put the madness to a halt, Oshodi was a community without rules.
Overcrowding was a pastime,
vehicles fighting for right of way,
traders and wares splattered around like water overflowing its riverbank.
Oshodi was the land of the dramatic,
with mundane happenings like a

man clutching so tightly to
his privates
to avoid the ones
who thrive on ill-gotten wealth,
to use it as an artefact for their own gain.
Oshodi was a land of four kings in
a deck of cards,
fighting for supremacy,
one king and several pawns emerging like
in a game of chess.
Oshodi was the aberration of what a
community should be, now finding its
way back to reckoning.

A molue is a long bus, with two columns of seats, that seats three people in one row and two on the other. These big yellow Lagos buses were very popular on Nigerian roads before the arrival of BRT buses.

Oshodi-Isolo is a local government area within Lagos State.

BAD MARKET

Lost in the howling sound of her voice,
vituperations like a soldier's bullet
in hushed tones, it was said
the absconding suitor who bolted out
    the left door dodged a bullet –
a bullet of heartache,
pain and anguish.

Her words were like a hunter's
arrow pointed to the kill;
her words were fire.
Her words undressed
the one who became her lot in the
    breaking of the day.
Her words stuck like glue on clay.

Adaobi was a *bad market,*
like untested electronics
sold in the dark of the night in Alaba
market.
Olatunde is desperate for heaven;

After all, life with Adaobi has been hell on Earth.

The term "Bad Market" was used as a metaphor in the poem.

Alaba International Market is an electronics market located in Ojo, Lagos State, Nigeria. It is the largest electronics market in Nigeria.

Adaobi is an Igbo name for girls meaning "first daughter of the royal palace (princess)".

Olatunde is a Yoruba name for boys, meaning "Wealth has come again".

MONEY LAUNDERING

Our customer due diligence is reactionary.
Our employees look the other way.
Every bank's dream is profit-making,
leaving smattering smiles on investors' faces.
We are at a crossroad,
out of control,
like a Formula One driver with eyes on the glory;
our internal controls have been thrown out the window.
We are brothers in arms
with the same criminals we seek to annihilate.
Regulatory fines are unending.
Like whiplash on a recalcitrant horse at the races,
our reputations have been damaged,
thrown into the gutter.
Ask Dance-kay,
the dancing masquerade in the village square mired

in the ocean of money laundering and the ill-wind we seek to abate. A cleaner
financial system is the goal,
an end to illicit funds, accessories to crime
and a safer financial system that is less lucrative
for money laundering.

DEADBEAT DAD

Being a super dad is not anomalous;

    it's in the little things – the
    loving, caring and listening.

Don't be a deadbeat dad.

Fatherhood is not plain sailing;
    there are tidal waves,
    tumultuous oceans
    and icebergs to rock the boat.

STIGMA

Kept in a silo,
hidden among the trenches,
the child of sorrow,
the unwanted one who is a curse,
a curse to the lineage
of astounding talent.
You have special needs,
thrust into a special school
to live an un-special life,
harried and bullied for a sin,
a sin I never knew about,
discoloured by the toga and
colouration of unwanted, abnormal
and shamed
by those who should help me live a normal life.
Your unsaid words were littered on your faces like a filthy toilet. I was the brunt of labels,
like a formatted memory stick.

Stigma was my companion;

Stigmatised was the only city I ever lived in.

Inspired by Fehintola Da-Silva – To everyone who has been stigmatised, you are not alone.

PAINED

You are not alone in the
 trauma that seems
 unending. We have
 eaten our fries with no
 mains.
Our friends have taunted us at
 the turn of the day and our
 fiery prayer points fall right on
 our faces.
Life is not fair.
It's not a fairy tale
or a Nollywood movie with so many
 twists and turns. But in this
 pain, I take solace
that I am not a wandering loner in the
 wilderness of life,
this wickedness that has now been a
 part of the journey.
I am pained, gutted
and disenchanted,
but I take solace knowing there will be
 an end someday.

THINGS WE SAY FOR LOVE

The conception of love in our minds
    as teenagers was a fairy tale.
As students from the school of the
    Mills & Boon book series,
    graduating in flying colours,
Romeo and Juliet were the golden
    source for what true love should
    be.
We made promises
that only remained in the realm of
promises –
I will serve you breakfast in bed
all of my life
or I will die for you
were some of the semantics that we
    sputtered before the veil of the
    allusions of false love was lifted
and the harsh realities of life
    dawned upon us.
I am still waiting to see a news
    headline in quick succession
for the person who died
for the one they truly loved or the

one
    who was served breakfast in bed all
        of their life in the name of love.
Things we could do for love have
        truly been unmasked,
as things we could say for love got
        watered down
and thrown onto the back burner
when the harsh realities of life
        dawned upon us.

THE RANDY MAN

For the extreme believer in the
matrimony of one man and wife, at
times polygamy is thrust upon us
by a philandering partner
or an abrasive one who tears
down without any fabric of
emotion.
No one set out to bring fire
so close to home
or be vulnerable to the arrow of
unfiltered words; Babatunde
was the nemesis of the young
girls.
We could be right – he was pushed
to the limits.
Ayomide, his wife, had a mouth
like the unrepaired tap in
the neighbourhood,
but he could do with some dignity,
a father figure who has figuratively
left a vacuum, lost his voice.
How can he open his mouth to tell off
Ewatomi's husband?

Who has found in him an alibi?

A worthy example to emulate –

not for those few worthy traits

but the unworthy ones,
like impregnating another
man's wife. Left red-faced
but acting pretty bold,
like a corrupt Nigerian governor
   with immunity,
the untouchable aura
till the next victim to add to his
   unsavoury collection of
   antiquated medals.
Karma found Babatunde out;
karma left him bruised and damaged
   when he was served in his own
   coin
   in his favourite dish.

Ayomide is a unisex Yoruba name, meaning "My joy has come".

Ewatomi is a Yoruba name for girls, meaning "Beauty is enough".

Babatunde is a male given name. In the Yoruba language, it means "Father returns", or "A Father has returned". This generally refers to a male ancestor such as a deceased father, grandfather, or great grandfather.

LIFE IS A TEACHER

Life is an unusual teacher,
a teacher that gives no handouts.
We face examinations without preparation
or the luxury of burning the midnight candle.
It might serve you an undesirable meal,
like a vegetarian served a meat baguette
on an evening date.
Whatever life serves you and fate thrusts upon you,
don't accept it like a defeated battalion
retreating from the war front;
after all, life is meant to teach us, shape us
and at times shake us to our limits.
Make your own sauce,
garnish it and enjoy the meal
without those words
and actions of those who, chest in arms,
mutter in the bustle of the evening breeze
and the silent echoes of the dark nights:
Whatever will be, will be;
it was all my fate.

HOME TRAINING

Home these days is no longer what it used to be.
It has become a shadow of itself,
the ghost of its past glory.
Home has been deserted,
identical to a farmland ravaged
    by rampaging Fulani
    herdsmen.
So, training in a deserted home seems
    a foregone conclusion.
There can't be training in a home of
    untrained adults
who have nothing to pass down except
    yelling at kids,
bolting out of the front door
    at the slightest
    irritation;
then the cycle continues –
more untrained adults
raising up kids
who become moral burdens to society.
Homes without training was the
    beginning of our hitches;

now we await a revival or
    society   comes   to
ruin.

RICH IN CASH, POOR IN PEOPLE

People are the currency you need to
 navigate through the rough
 edges that life might throw your
 way.
You might be rich in cash
and your bank balance fat;
being poor in people means you are
 living on the cliff edge,
on the tenterhooks.
When we pass through the tunnel
or become lost in the dark alleyway –
these are riddles money can't solve.
Or our aeroplane is hit mid-air by
 severe turbulence,
that our hearts find a home in our
mouths –
people will come through in the air,
 the hostess conversing about
 survival strategies –
that might sound like a beginner
 learning a foreign language.
You can't survive without a nucleus.
There are days when money can't

save you from those pitfalls and
the emptiness of life stares us in
the eye like a motionless snail.
That is when we need our bank to be
filled with people,
humans with blood flowing through
their veins;
not your bundle of naira notes, your
pounds nor dollars will wipe
your slate clean.

Inspired by Moses Erim

GALLANT WARRIORS

Fighting in the World War,
we remember your heroics,
spilled blood
and the life you gave.
You were brave,
soldiered on.
We call you our heroes,
lest we forget
all the good works.
We will always remember you,
our gallant warriors.

For the heroes who fought in the World War and paid the ultimate price with their life

ONCE UPON A TIME (2)

The world has gone digital;
technological advancement has taken us in leaps and bounds;
technology has broken down limitations,
boundaries and barriers.
Once upon a time, our televisions were black and white. Colour television was a dream only in our fancies.
Once upon a time,
Facebook was only a dream in Zuckerberg's mind; Twitter, Instagram and WhatsApp are the reigning champions,
but remember – it's all fleeting.
Ask Blackberry.
Their story leaves a bad taste like a sour berry.
Once upon a time, our phones were not smart;
we used phones with no i's.
Nokia

was a nuclear power in its own right.
Once upon a time,
in some parts of the world, lanterns
and kerosene oil illuminated our
houses from the darkness of the
night.
As students, we burnt the midnight
candle,
yet we were trailblazers.
The world has grown in leaps and
bounds. Electric cars
and driverless cars are the new "in"
thing.
The world has gone mental,
but in it all, don't forget *you*.
Don't lose yourself –
your identity
in the new world of glamour kings
and queens
who, in truth, are far from
glamourous.
Don't lose yourself in the craziness of
this world. It's not a crime to be
unsociable,
to stand for values, dignity and

honour.

It's not a crime to marry as a virgin; neither is it a crime to uphold the values of respect for self and others.

Always remember – nothing lasts forever.

Inspired by Ayodeji Omogunsoye

INGRATE

Lending a helping hand can
    sometimes lead to a fatal end,
an apocalyptic reversal by
    ungrateful hearts
that etch their footprints all
    around the universe.
You can't satisfy humans who
    look to hide their feelings
behind the veil of a friend who
    didn't help enough
or an uncle that was just not
there.
Fanning the embers of hate,
we dig deep into the cesspit of
bitterness
to hide the scars of our
    vulnerability when we fell
    asleep,
left in a deep slumber while life
    happened in our absence,
the only seed we have to sow is
the seed of malevolence, odium,
    and antipathy. We spend our

adulthood as walking time-
bombs, like those moribund
buses
with nowhere to go except our
hate-filled hearts.

GLASS HOUSE

A sage once said,
Those who make glass houses
    their habitat never fling stones.
I once lived in a glass house.
With a penchant for gravitating
    towards stones, I threw words,
    mortar and bricks.
Like a reverberating sound bar,
everyone was shook,
their table never remained the
    same.
It's all right to swim against the
    tide,
go against the waves
and the sage,
creaking aloud like a car
with a faulty silencer on Third
    Mainland Bridge.
History can be re-written,
a new voice emerging from the
    woods.

CHRISTMAS

Christmas is a season of firecrackers –
we don't eat no crackers.
Forget the cheese;
spreading love
like an almond butter spread on my
    parched brown bread.
Christmas is in asunder,
broken without Christ in the
    centre, comparable to an
    unsolved maths formula riddle
or a deserted M-and-S building on a
    snowy morning
or a sombre mass after a
    destructive rainstorm.
    Christmas is the time
without motion,
food decimated in reckless
    abandon, no input on a tracker,
no timelord overlooking my broad
    shoulders like a car tailgate on
    the Silverlink. Christmas is that
    time to share built-up love, not

hours.

We had an August visitor
who overlooked August.
Christ came in December with
love. Merry Christmas.

*Jesus is the reason for the season –
do not water it down. There is no
Christmas without Christ.*

FRUITION

Fruition was the fruit of intuition. The Cokers are straight forward – we don't play no poker.

Fruition was the seed of a dream;

now reality stares you in the face

like a wide-eyed eagle

We all dream;

bringing an idea to fruition is noble.

In the heart of Barking,

we are a powerhouse,

durable like a Hummer jeep.

Once low rank,

now game changers –

flying so high, like Power Rangers, against all odds.

Accounting is our minimum;

excellence is our normal.

Dedicated to Abiodun Coker, CEO of Fruition Consultants, an accounting firm renowned for excellence.

ROCCAGORGA

In Roccagorga,

I had a date with destiny;

I had a date with a family who

shared the same name with my

heritage.

They gave me a stage,

to shine and illuminate;

a plate of Italian pizza;

a chance to enlighten and roar

with tsars and empresses.

We roared in joy,

somewhere in Emmaus Christian

School,

a home of the future,

dreams so big no one can rupture.

I believe in the future;

I believe in the next generation.

Rhoda, Phebe and Mary

are my sisters from another

mother.

You only need one chance,

a date with destiny,

a stage and voice,

to give others the chance
to find their own unique roar.

Dedicated to the Akinyemi's and the amazing students of Emmaus Christian School that I met in December 2018 in Roccagorga, Italy.

CULTURE

Don't forget your culture,
as you might end up with tough luck.
It is immaturity to get lost in another city,
with their waning ethos and values.
How do you explain to a little one
values so endearing in the place you once called home?
Your culture is your stamp post,
tattooed on your arms like a signature on a bank draft.
Don't get carried away like a car with no satellite navigation.
You can't be more British than Britons;
neither can you be more Catholic than the pope.
Embrace your culture.
Let it be your identity.
Be culturally minded.

MAGICAL

We all need that moment of magic –

when we can flick a trick,

do the surreal,

even when we know it's unreal.

Be magical. Do the impossible.

Give that stumbling block a finishing punch,

like Scorpion in a Mortal Kombat game.

Hug the finish line in ecstasy.

Don't settle for indolence.

Be magical.

Dedicated to Jack Stephenson

WISDOM

We were like lambs in the midst of wolves;
we hugged wisdom so tight.
We dined with our frenemies at the same table.
They took our names to the slaughter lab, blood dripping from their mouths.
We borrowed a leaf from the serpent and dove. Wisdom has to be the partner.
Ask T'Challa in *Black Panther*.
In a world full of backstabbers and gossips,
many are like rudderless ships, caught in a vicious cycle of hate and bitterness. Friends are for seasons –
comparable to my favourite manager, Jose Mourinho, who has never lasted four seasons in a club.
Get insight.

With all of your being, hunt it.
Park the bus when you need to –
that's wisdom.
There will be days when you need
to attack, attack and attack,
singing *Ole, Ole, Ole.*
That's the conclusion of the
matter – get wise!

Frenemies is an abbreviation for
Friends like enemies.

THIRTY-FIVE THOUSAND FEET

Flying at thirty-five thousand feet
    above sea level sends me into
    fits of fear,
cold shivers and jitters with every
    turbulent wind.
The demonstrations by the air
    hostess are, at best, half-
    hearted;
Every announcement from the
    pilot's cockpit
sends me into a frenzy,
    palpitations and deep
    reflection.
Don't blame me for building a
    home in the garden of fear and
    watering it with the seeds of
    an ill-fated crash.
I detest being a headline on a
    major news channel for
    specious reasons;
it might be my chance to hug the
    limelight for leading over a
    hundred souls to heaven's

gate;
or say a prayer in my hour of need
    for a divine turnaround and
    the incredible becoming
    conceivable.
I could as well, in cowardice, say
    my last prayer, accepting this
    as my fate,
as my faith barometer would, at
    best, be at its lowest ebb when
    I journey to high altitudes
and land in one piece.
I am filled with unfathomable
    gratitude for not being a
    statistic
in the catalogue of human errors:
    a defective engine
or a pilot who wants to end it all.
    We all detest a crash;
no one likes to be fed as a carcass
    to the birds
or fishes that look for what to prey
    on in the Mediterranean Sea
and Atlantic Ocean. Flying at
    thirty-five thousand feet

tosses me into fits of fear

that could only be resolved by a

    dosage of faith.

KING

I am a king,
a wordsmith with rhymes.
So sleek.

As a mentor, my writing gifts speak volumes.

A hero.
Look at me – I came from ground zero.
I am creative
and I don't need your affirmation.

I am a victor.
My failures are stepping stones. I am a king.
Give me the crown. It fits perfectly.

DON'T ENVY

Don't envy. Everyone has their season.

Keep on striving.
Life is all about timing,
just keep climbing,
eyes on the goal.
Someday you will be at the topmost.

Walk around with a smile. Don't be vile;
erase bitterness and its concubines.

Envy is a cancer; being bitter
can leave you dirty, like littered
streets. Embrace peace. Don't live
in strife.
Everyone has a chance to have a
    pop at the top
and at greatness.

CONTENDER

I was once a pretender; now a contender,
my words are so tender.

I was once in the shadow.
Look at me shining so bright, like
a rainbow radiating a special glow.

I was once forgotten; saved by the begotten,
you would think I had just won
the lottery.

I am the resolute defender,
so strong. Like the recession-hit
money-lender, I am here to stay

for good.

GOSSIP

Like roads thawing, clutching at
straws;
like workmen drilling at the village
borehole, no water in sight,
we converge like streams looking
for who to wash down, our
tongues like fiery darts
leading us astray, like a missing
hunter's dog in the thick
forest. We are on the lookout
for dirty laundry.
We have more news material than
the local tabloid. Our smiles
are mired in deceit.
We are backbiters, masters of
assumptions,
pre-emptions and insinuations.
What you need might be
therapeutic,
healing. Let go
and truly live your life.
Remember – idle talk abides in the
camp of idle minds.

TIT FOR TAT

Tit for tat is the name of the game.
    Hear my epiphany
and take heed –
we are conjoined like Siamese
    twins with the vengeful at
    heart. Our hearts are habitat
    for war.
Your unsaid words were arrow
    darts piercing my skin.
Your expressions were the final
    jigsaws
in the puzzle of those who saw
    you through a needle's eye. An
    eye for an eye
only left two one-eyed folks or two
    blind people,
blinded by having a way which led
    to nowhere. Choose your
    battles wisely.
Tit for tat,
a tooth for a tooth only leaves
    broken pieces
that may never get fixed again.

DEAD LIONS DON'T ROAR 2

We roared like lions;
never forget the barking dogs,
like revving cars in the parking lot.
True kings don't cower;
they stand tall like the Burj Khalifa,
reaching for the sun like a flower.
Let me water you into your own promised land –
bloom in the morning,
radiate at noon,
shine brightly with the evening moon. Unleash your creative juices like Fela, the king of Afrobeat. Let me saturate you with my words,
roar and voice.
Let the lion in me fire you awakening shots to wake

up your giant.
Let my life be the torch
that will spark you into your own revelation.
Let these verses evoke emotions so deep. Remember – sleeping dreams do no good. Paper warriors are mere artefacts.
Pour out your greatness like libations;

let my books and flowery cantos intoxicate you
till you stagger into your own greatness. Reminisce on this all day long:
dead lions don't roar. Roar and don't stop roaring.

Inspired by Oloyede Michael Taiwo (Alias Philo Baba

EXHALE

Exhale and inhale,
breathe the sound of life into those lifeless objects, like the three statues screaming "Welcome to Lagos".
Labet makes art;
Labet makes stunning art, turning the innocuous to dazzling.
Labet stimulates life into those lifeless artefacts.
I will exhale and dance to the rhythm of Labet;
I will inhale the new life with a rhythm to my dance steps and a swagger unseen.
I will march like a five-star general who has just led a battalion to triumph.
I will embrace creativity like a love-smitten bachelor. Labet makes top-notch art;
Labet makes illustrations that whisper with silent timbres.

Labet is the Afroqueen
with the Midas touch and golden fingers.

Dedicated to the exceptionally talented Lola Betiku of Labetmakesart

MY WORDS

Don't read between the lines.

My words are my talents, expressed.

There are times I am cruising on a high,

like a plane flying through the night sky.

Other times, I am on a low,

like a convalescing man on the riverbank.

My words are fictional,

even though they may hit you in the hub of your heart, prickling your conscience.

Let my words serenade you, comforting you with the warmest of hugs.

Bio

Tolu' A. Akinyemi (also known as Tolutoludo & Lion of Newcastle) is a multi-award-winning Nigerian author in the genre of poetry, short story, children's literature and essays. His works include: *Dead Lions Don't Roar* (poetry, 2017), *Unravel Your Hidden Gems* (essays, 2018), *Dead Dogs Don't Bark* (poetry, 2018), *Dead Cats Don't Meow* (poetry, 2019), *Never Play Games with the Devil* (poetry, 2019), *Inferno of Silence* (short stories, 2020), *A Booktiful Love* (poetry, 2020), *Black ≠ Inferior* (poetry, 2021), *Never Marry a Writer* (poetry, 2021), *Everybody Don Kolomental* (poetry, 2021), *I Wear Self-Confidence Like a Second Skin* (children's literature, 2021), *I Am Not a Troublemaker* (children's literature, 2021), *Born in Lockdown* (poetry, forthcoming – September 2021) and *A god in a human body* (poetry, forthcoming – January 2022).

Tolu' has been endorsed by the Arts Council England as a writer with "exceptional talent". A former headline act at Great Northern Slam, Crossing the Tyne Festival, and Feltonbury Arts and Music Festival, he also inspires large audiences through spoken word performances. He has appeared as a keynote speaker in major forums and events and facilitates creative writing master classes to many audiences.

His poems have appeared in the 57th issue (Volume 15, no 1) of the *Wilderness House Literary Review*, *The Writers Cafe Magazine* Issue 18, GN Books, Lion and Lilac, and elsewhere.

His books are based on a deep reality and often reflect relationships and life and features people he has met in his journey as a writer. His books have inspired many people to improve their performance and/or their circumstances. Tolu' has taken his poetry to the stage, performing his written word at many events. Through his writing and these performances, he supports business leaders, other aspiring authors, and people of all ages interested in reading and writing. Sales of the books have allowed Tolu' to donate to charity, allowing him to make a difference where he feels it is important, and to show that he lives by the words he puts to the page.

He is a co-founder of Lion and Lilac, a UK-based arts organisation and sits on the board of many organisations.

Tolu' is a financial crime consultant as well as a Certified Anti-Money Laundering Specialist (CAMS) with extensive experience working with leading investment banks and consultancy firms.

He is a trained economist from Ekiti State University, formerly known as University of Ado-Ekiti (UNAD). He sat for his master's degree in Accounting and Financial Management at the University of Hertfordshire, Hatfield, United Kingdom. Tolu' was a student ambassador at the University of Hertfordshire, Hatfield, representing the university in major forums and engaging with young people during various assignments.

Tolu' Akinyemi was born in Ado-Ekiti, Nigeria and lives in the United Kingdom. He is an ardent supporter of Chelsea Football Club in London.

You can connect with Tolu' on his various social media accounts:

Instagram: @ToluToludo

Facebook: facebook.com/toluaakinyemi

Twitter: @ToluAkinyemi

Author's Note

Thank you for the time you have taken to read this book. I hope you enjoyed the poems in it.

If you loved the book and have a minute to spare, I would appreciate a short review on the page or site where you bought it. I greatly appreciate your help in promoting my work. Reviews from readers like you make a huge difference in helping new readers choose a book.

                    Thank you!
                  Tolu' Akinyemi

Dead Lions Don't Roar

In a society where moral rectitude is increasingly becoming abeyant, Akinyemi's bounden duty is to reawaken it with verses. He, thus, functions as a philosopher-poet, a kind of factotum inculcating wisdom in different facets of life. *Dead Lions Don't Roar* leads us into the universe of an exact mind rousing the lethargic from indolence or prevarication, bearing in mind that the greatest achievers are those who take the bull by the horn. Taking a step can just be the open sesame to reach the stars. Enough of jeremiad! – **The Sun**

Dead Lions Don't Roar, a collection of poetic wisdom for the discerning, makes an interesting read. A paper pack, the poems are concise, easy to digest, travel friendly and express deep feelings and noble thoughts in beautiful and simple language. – **The Nation**

Akinyemi's verses are concise, straight-edge and explanatory, reminiscent of the kind of poetry often churned out by Mamman J. Vatsa, the late soldier and poet. – **yNaija**

Dead Lion's Don't Roar is a collection of inspiring and motivating modern-day verses. Addressing many issues close to home and also many taboo subjects, the poems reflect today's struggles and light the way to a positive future. This uplifting book will appeal to all age groups and anyone going through change, building or enjoying a career, or facing day-to-day struggles. Many of the short verses will resonate with readers, leaving them with a sense of peace and well-being.

Dead Dogs Don't Bark

Dead Dogs Don't Bark is as culturally relevant as can be, and this deserves commendation. – **Bellanaija**

In a nutshell, Dead Dogs Don't Bark is enjoyable, it is stimulating. - **Bdaily UK**

The collection takes this reader through an exhilarating journey of wits and pun. The power of words, both grand and subtle, is that it allows the reader to place himself in the scheme and feel the poems on a more visceral level.
Creating concrete imageries, the poet says even before it sticks out its tongue and bares its teeth, the first thing that defeats a fainthearted in an unfamiliar threshold is the bark of a dog. It sends cold shivers running down the spine. That very bark, disarming as

it is, is the dog's way of calling attention: I am here! - **Guardian Arts**

Dead Dogs Don't Bark is the second poetry collection from the acclaimed author Tolu' A. Akinyemi. With a similar tone and style to *Dead Lions Don't Roar* (Tolu's first poetry collection), this follow-up masterpiece is nothing short of pure motivation.

The poems cover a range of topics that many in life are aware of, that the author himself has experienced, and that we all, whatever our age, need support in. Beautifully written, the poems speak volumes to all age groups as they encourage finding your inner talent and celebrating your individuality and distinct voice.

The poetry collection contains didactic elements for negating the effects of peer pressure and criminality, along with many other forces. Also covering mental health, relationships, career focus, and general life issues, the poetry is, in turn, bittersweet, amusing and thought-provoking.

Dead Cats Don't Meow

In all, this poetry collection *Dead Cats Don't Meow* generally emphasizes the theme of self-belief and taking action. It reminds me of the saying "if you think you are too little to make an impact, try staying in a room with a mosquito." - **BellaNaija.**

Overall, *Dead Cats Don't Meow* comes across as a collection of thoughtful poetry that inspires, entertains, and educates its reader. It is a great blend of themes spanning across love, inspiration, politics, entrepreneurship, marriage and life, among others. Its simplicity eludes intentionality, and the plays on words show experience.

The collection is suitable for both the literary and non-literary community and is a great work for all manner of readers.

I believe, with this one, Akinyemi has achieved his goals of motivation.
- **The Nation Newspaper.**

Dead Cats Don't Meow urges its readers not to waste their ninth life... the author of this collection of poetic wisdom for the discerning adds his third compendium of poems to the bookshelves alongside *Dead Lions Don't Roar* and *Dead Dogs Don't Bark*. Tolu' A. Akinyemi, renowned poet, author and performer, brings to us *Dead Cats Don't Meow*, a metrical masterpiece which invokes love and respect for life with every word. Each poem examines a part of life, a sensation, a reaction, or an emotion. Beautifully written... individually, the verses breathe their own beat, whilst the collection knits together perfectly to present an idyllic collection to attain innate potential. Don't waste the ninth life! Don't miss the chance to add this rare compendium of poetic wisdom to your bookshelf today!

Unravel Your Hidden Gems

Unravel Your Hidden Gems is like a Solomon talking to us in the 21st century. The book teaches us to value what we have, the pursuit of excellence, and, above all, steps to unravel your hidden gems, drawn from your extraordinary talents, deposited in you right from the first day the placenta was severed from the womb. A book for all seasons, no doubt, especially in Africa where aspirations sometimes do not match inspirations, it is only logical that you add it to your shopping cart. - **Guardian Arts**

Watching others ascend the totem pole of life with relative ease, some come to believe they can't fly. Times without number, they have tried, yet they have found no way to break the ice. Don't despair if you are unsettled by a losing streak.

Tolu Akinyemi, the author of *Unravel Your Hidden Gems,* believes that the hero lies in you. If only you can discover the hidden gems in you, you are on your way to excelling. How, then, do you dig deep into the labyrinth for the gems?

Unravel Your Hidden Gems is a 376-page book by a prolific UK-based Nigerian author. It is a collection of over 360 inspirational and motivational essays from a young man who feels he has a mission to rouse dampened spirits to make the much-needed push in life to regenerate abundantly.

In seven parts, the author makes a diligent search into typical problems encountered by men, capable of weighing them down, and comes up with snippets of wisdom. - **The Sun**

Unravel Your Hidden Gems is a collection of inspirational and motivational essays from the heart of the acclaimed author, Tolu' A. Akinyemi. Released hot on the heels of Tolu's first book of poetry, *Dead Lions Don't Roar,* this new book is a study on life, encouraging people to succeed at what they feel is important to their own happiness – be it their private life, business, religion, career, or relationships; each part of life is discovered. This mind-altering life manual can be read as a whole or visited in snippets for day-to-day inspiration. Each essay examines and highlights challenges in life and how to succeed in enjoying life with grace. A self-help study on life with a refreshing difference, the book is a totality of life's journey, reminding us we are here on a temporary basis and that it is our duty to not hide in obscurity, but to *Unravel Your Hidden Gems* before it is too late! Pure Inspiration!

Never Play Games with the Devil

Reflective, insightful, and ultimately inspirational, *Never Play Games with the Devil* is a collection best digested slowly and thoughtfully. It's a series of insights and admonitions about life's purposes and coping mechanisms for *"...not crashing under the weight of the world."*
D. Donovan, Senior Reviewer, Midwest Book Review

Readers will find Akinyemi's reflections on significant life issues completely relevant, sharply logical, and deeply felt. - **The Prairies Book Review**

Hear the poet as, in a succinct moment of self-adulation, he writes:

> My brain thinks faster than my words can convey.
> My mind works magic. Can I live this life forever?

Divided into three sections, *Never Play Games with the Devil* showcases a poet at the height of his powers, exploring several themes in different voices.

In the first section, the poet is the charismatic preacher encouraging people to hustle, find their feet and grow. He writes about the lot of broken men crashing under the weight of expectations; he talks about boys like Eddie and Edmund, bullied for the shape of their heads. He humorously addresses the consequence of choices in the title poem, *Never Play Games with the Devil*.

The second section secures him a seat as an activist. We see the poet tackle, in verse, despotic and undemocratic governments, marauding killer herdsmen, and the pastor who lost his voice. The poet mourns the hapless souls in the crossfire between society's rot and the State's insouciance.

The final poems explore the basis of human relationships. The poems here deal with love, commitment and trust.

Never Play Games with the Devil is a didactic collection of poems on pertinent life issues. These poems draw their appeal from the poet's ability to sustain a figment of thought through the entire span of each poem.

A Booktiful Love

Poet Tolu' A. Akinyemi tackles life with a passionate, analytical, observing eye and creates admonitions which pull at emotional strings in the heart. Poetry readers who choose his free verse collection will find it equally powerful whether it's considering divorce and grief or the love language of 'A Booktiful Love'. - **D. Donovan - Senior Reviewer, Midwest Book Review.**

Readers will find Akinyemi's collection an intriguing approach to exploration of the entirety of human experience in its various forms. This is a superb collection. - **The Prairies Book Review.**

A Booktiful Love is a collection of poems that deal with the entirety of human experience in its various forms. Didactically rich, the poems explore ideas ranging from love, relationships and patriotism to marriage, morality and many other concepts pertinent to daily living.

Given its variety of themes, what unifies the poems in this collection is the simplicity and ambiguousness of language that the poet employs. The poems draw their strength from their clarity and meaning.

These are poems with a purpose. Poet Tolu' A. Akinyemi doesn't shy away from this fact, as he writes in the poems *Writers* and *Write for Rights*. The poet's philosophy is evident in this collection. To him, a writer is saddled with the responsibility to use his words to teach, preach and fight for freedom.

He writes:

> *Let's change the world, one writer at a time, write those words till the world gets it right.*

Another special attribute to this collection is the poet's experimentation with words. This is clear right from the title. The poet identifies himself as a creator of words. The reader is obliged to travel into the mind of the writer in each poem, to understand how his mind works. As readers approach the end of this collection, they not only become engrossed in its didactic richness, but will also appreciate the uniqueness of the poet's style and the sense of responsibility he carries.

Inferno of Silence

Inferno of Silence is a wide-ranging collection that tackles different themes of love, life, interpersonal relationships, and social and political challenges. It's a hard-hitting, revealing collection that keeps readers engaged and thinking with each short exploration of characters who confront their prejudices, realities, and the winds of change in their lives.

Readers of literary explorations that include African cultural influence and modern-day dilemmas will find this collection engrossing. - **D. Donovan, Senior Reviewer, Midwest Book Review**

Poignant and honest...

Akinyemi's first collection of short stories dazzles with elegant prose, genuine emotions, and Nigerian cultural lore as it plumbs both the socio-cultural issues and the depths of love, loss, grief, and personal trauma. Lovers of literary fiction will be rewarded. - **The Prairies Book Review**

The first collection of short stories by this multitalented author entwines everyday events that are articulated in excellent storytelling.

The title story *Inferno of Silence* portrays men's societal challenges and the unspoken truths and burdens that men bear, while *Black Lives Matter* shows the firsthand trauma of a man facing racism as a footballer plying his trade in Europe.

Stories range from *Return Journey*, where we encounter a techpreneur/ poet/serial womanizer confronting consequences of his past actions, to *Blinded by Silence*, where a couple united by love must face a political upheaval changing their fortune.

These are completed with stories of relationships: *Trouble in Umudike* – about family wealth and marriage; *Everybody don Kolomental*, where the main character deals with mental health issues; and *In the Trap of Seers*, when one's life is on auto-reverse with the death of her confidante, her mother, as she takes us through her ordeal and journey to redemption.
This is a broad and very inclusive collection.

BLACK ≠INFERIOR

Akinyemi employs a steady hand and heart to capturing Black lives in various nuances, from political and social arenas to personal experience: *"Equality is a forgotten child. The blood of the innocents/soil the World. Racial Injustice walks tall,/the graves of our ancestors quake in anguish/at this perpetual ignominy."*

This juxtaposition of the personal and the political makes *Black#Inferior* a particularly important read. It holds a compelling, accessible message to the Black community in the form of hard-hitting poems which offer emotional observations of the modern state of Black minds and societies around the world.

Poetry readers interested in the fusion of literary

ability and social inspection will appreciate the hard-hitting blend of both in Black#Inferior, which is recommended reading for a wide audience, especially students of Black experience.- D. Donovan - Senior Reviewer, Midwest Book Review.

A celebration of black culture and experience and life in general, the collection makes for an electrifying read. - The Prairies Book Review.

Black ≠ Inferior is a collection of poems divided into 2 parts. The first part is a collection of thematically linked poems exploring Blackness and the myriads of issues it attracts. The second part oscillates themes—talking about consent, a query of death, a celebration of love among others. In his usual stylistic, this collection deals with weighty matters like race and colourism with simple and clear language.

In Black ≠ Inferior, we see Tolu' Akinyemi reacting in response to the world, to issues that affect Black people. Here, we see a poet shedding off his burdens through his poems; hence, the beauty of this collection is in the issues it attempts to address. In this collection, Tolu' wears a coat of many colours – he is a preacher, a prophet, a doctor and a teacher.

We see Tolu' the preacher in these lines:
'I wish you can rise through the squalor of poverty
  and voices that watercolour you as under-represented.
I wish you can emblaze your name in gold,
and swim against every wave of hate.'

This is a collection of poems fit for the present narrative as any (Black) person who reads this collection should beam with confidence at the end.

This is what the poet sets out to achieve with his oeuvre.

NEVER MARRY A WRITER

Ultimately, the poet's caution to "Never Marry a Writer" is a deeper disclaimer, a warning that is more a promise. Writers, these poems remind the reader, bear witness. Whether evocative prose or colorful whimsy or the bleakest of forthright documentation, their words attest to the truths they observe. With its wily wordy ways, this collection reminds readers that even those without a literary spouse are nevertheless subject to--and on notice from--those who, like the author, observe and document. --- "The US Review of Books" (RECOMMENDED by the US Review)

"Bold, wry, and lyrical musings." -- *Kirkus Reviews*

OH, THE WEBS WE WEAVE...

For his seventh poetry collection, Tolu' has turned his attention to that old adage -
no one in a writer's life may have secrets.
A vibrant, human exploration of the way in which words and deeds connect all of us, and the tiniest movements which span out across continents.

Tolu' writes powerfully on family, love, loss, and with a scorching curiosity for the world around us. His readers will be familiar with his inimitable style, and this latest collection does not disappoint.

EVERYBODY DON KOLOMENTAL

At its core, the work is simply authentic and resonates both for its content and style. Delivering an almost lyrical sensation with the combination of smaller stanzas, the author's poetry references a multitude of life circumstances, including but not limited to middle school, therapy, and bachelorhood. Filled with poems that unveil a new gem of realization upon each subsequent reading, Akinyemi's poetry is a sure-fire must-read. --- "The US Review of Books". --- "The US Review of Books" (RECOMMENDED by the US Review)

A poignant collection that captures both the raw sorrows and joys of human existence.... --- "The Prairies Book Review"
Hope is Not Far Away...

Everybody Don Kolomental is a collection of poems that deal with everyday universal struggles.

Tolu' peddles hope to the lost and hopeless and pulls at the emotional strings of the heart in this collection of heartfelt poems. The collection mirrors life through the eyes of a deep-thinker and wordsmith.

Poet Tolu' A. Akinyemi knows the gravity of mental health struggles and uses his words as a soothing balm to heal readers of this collection.

In the poem titled 'Hope is not Far Away', he writes:

"Who will tell Okikiola that hope is not far away?

Its ship docked in the home of Akinyele before his candle was blown out and his flailing dreams were a shipwreck.

Who will tell Okikiola this is not the last straw?

These wind gusts would give way for the calming sea."

Whether you're in need of calm after the storm, therapy, healing, or to view everyday struggles from the lens of a veteran poet, this collection is for you.

A god IN A HUMAN BODY

Tolu' A. Akinyemi is a philosopher-poet and a deep thinker, and his journey into the realm of the spiritual would leave readers in awe.

A god in a human body is Tolu' A. Akinyemi's ninth poetry collection.

This collection is a meditation on the fleeting nature of human life. A god in a human body explores themes of spirituality, divinity and the enormous power that we possess while we traverse this earthly passage.

A god in a human body will take you on a rollercoaster of emotions and its pages will leave readers craving for more.

I AM NOT A TROUBLEMAKER

Chadwick has just joined a new school, and he is stung by the label of troublemaker.

Will the label stick, or will he get the chance to come clean?

I WEAR SELF-CONFIDENCE LIKE A SECOND SKIN

Matilda has been battling her fears at home and in school.

Will she be able to build her self-confidence or will she crumble under the weight of her fears?

www.ingramcontent.com/pod-product-compliance
Lightning Source LLC
Chambersburg PA
CBHW021437080526
44588CB00009B/559